History of the CHILI Crossroads Bible Church

Dr. A. Joseph Essington

Retired • Teacher • Chaplain

Gotham Books

30 N Gould St.
Ste. 20820, Sheridan, WY 82801
https://gothambooksinc.com/

Phone: 1 (307) 464-7800

© 2024 *Dr. A. Joseph Essington.* All rights reserved.

No part of this book may be reproduced, stored in a retrieval system, or transmitted by any means without the written permission of the author.

Published by Gotham Books (May 29, 2024)

ISBN: 979-8-88775-973-9 (H)
ISBN: 979-8-88775-886-2 (P)
ISBN: 979-8-88775-887-9 (E)

Because of the dynamic nature of the Internet, any web addresses or links contained in this book may have changed since publication and may no longer be valid.

The views expressed in this work are solely those of the author and do not necessarily reflect the views of the publisher, and the publisher hereby disclaims any responsibility for them.

DEDICATION

To the Faithful Pastors and Board Members, who have served Chili Crossroads Bible Church and its congregation over the years, and particularly to the sacred memory of:

MICHAEL LOUIS IANNIELLO
March 29, 1953 - November 25, 2012

This highly respected Christian Husband, Father, Grandfather, Businessman, Church Board Chairman, and Friend, was greatly used of the LORD in this church's transitioning from its old building to its modern new facility.

TABLE OF CONTENTS

INTRODUCTION 1

Chapter 1

    The Church in Its Historical Setting (1783-1879) 3

Chapter 2

    The Legacy of St. John's German Evangelical Church Congregation of Chili, Coshocton County, Ohio (1879-1953) 8

Chapter 3

    The Reopening of the Old Church at the Crossroads The Pastorate of Rev. Owen E. Lower (1953-1961) 14

Chapter 4

    Chili Crossroads Bible Church Matures and Becomes Completely Independent The Pastorate of Rev. James H. Boyd (1961-1983) 17

Chapter 5

    The Chili Congregation's Ministry As A Strong Vibrant Bible Church (1983-2004) 21

Chapter 6

    The LORD'S Great Answers to Sincere Prayer at Chili (2004-2009) 25

Chapter 7

    The Preparatory Ministry of Pastor Joseph Essington (Spring - Summer - Fall, 2009) 33

Chapter 8

    An Active Growing Church with a Vision for the Future The Ongoing Ministry of Pastor Neal and Julie Dearyan (2009-Present) 41

APPENDIX 50

EPILOGUE 51

CONCLUSION 52

BIBLIOGRAPHY

    Pamphlets, Magazines, Newspapers: 54

    Valuable Internet Sources: 54

ACKNOWLEDGMENTS 55

INDEX 56

INTRODUCTION

*Now go, write it before them in a table, and note it in a book,
that it may be for the time to come for ever and ever. Isaiah 30.8*

The Chili Crossroads Bible Church is a local assembly of Christian believers, which has its spiritual roots deep in the pages of the New Testament. Indeed, when this church was founded, it was patterned after the original church in Jerusalem, described in Acts chapters 2 and 4. The Chili assembly began under the leadership of a capable missionary pastor — a church planter — as did most of the churches mentioned in the New Testament.

This book is about the Chili Crossroads Bible Church. It has been written to document its history, and in so doing, to honor and glorify the one true and living Triune God — Father, Son, and Holy Spirit — Who in His Wise Providence led true believers to come together to form this church. And He has abundantly blessed this local church for more than sixty years!

This book has also been written to encourage readers who are Christian believers to be faithful to the Chili Crossroads Bible Church — and to other churches of like precious faith — as these believers realize that our Lord has so wonderfully blessed this local church located in east-central Ohio, and He is prepared to bless other churches as well.

Another reason for the writing of this book has been to encourage any readers, who do not have a credible faith in the Lord Jesus Christ as Personal Savior, to believe on Him, and be saved (Acts 16:31), since this is the most important decision in life that any person can ever make (John 1:12, Acts 4:12).

And, finally, this book has been written to help its readers gain a better understanding of the history of the Chili Crossroads Bible Church — including the church's historical roots in the past, where the church is at the present time, and the direction the church is heading in, as it moves into the future.

Some words of explanation about Chapters One and Two of this book are in order. The first chapter of this book was written to explain the historical background of the chapters that follow. Chapter One begins with the Year 1783, when the Treaty of Paris of 1783 was signed. The Revolutionary War in America was fought from 1775-1781, and the Treaty of Paris of 1783 was the agreement signed by delegates from Great Britain, France, the newly formed United States, and Spain to resolve the issues which led to that war. A provision of that Treaty gave the land north of the Ohio River to the United States. That provision resulted in Americans and Europeans settling the Ohio Territory, and Ohio becoming the 17th State in the United States in 1803. Coshocton County in the State of Ohio was then organized in 1811, and Crawford Township in Coshocton County, where the church is located, was incorporated in 1828.

The second chapter of this book begins with the Year 1879 by presenting a historical description of St. John's German Evangelical Church Congregation of Chili in Crawford Township, Ohio. That church was formed in the year 1879 and permanently closed its doors in 1947, but its assets, including its land, its cemetery, its church building, and most of its remaining personal property and artifacts were later transferred to the Chili Crossroads Bible Church. Most of these assets are still owned by the Chili Crossroads Bible Church today.

Chapters Three through Seven continue with much of the history of the church, and Chapter Eight tells of the wonderful ways in which the LORD is blessing the church under the ministry of Pastor Neal Dearyan and his wife, Julie.

For the author, it has been a genuine privilege to work with the Chili Crossroads Bible Church, and it is his earnest prayer that our GREAT ETERNAL GOD AND SAVIOR, the LORD OF HISTORY and THE LORD OF HIS CHURCH, will continue to bless this wonderful local assembly of believers, and that He will bless every individual who reads this book in part or in whole.

Dr. A. Joseph Essington
Carneys Point, New Jersey
July 2013

Chapter 1

The Church in Its Historical Setting (1783-1879)

And (God) hath made of one blood all nations of men to dwell on the face of the earth, and hath determined the times before appointed and the boundaries of their habitation...
Acts 17:26

The United States acquired Ohio from Great Britain when the American Revolutionary War ended. The British surrendered at Yorktown, VA on October 17, 1781. Peace talks began in Paris in 1782. In September 1783, the delegates of four nations — the United States, Great Britain, France, and Spain — signed the Treaty of Paris, which confirmed U.S. independence and set the boundaries of the new nation. The United States then stretched from the Atlantic Ocean to the Mississippi River and from Canada to the Florida border.

Traveling north into Chili years ago on the unpaved road (now County Road 10)
Note: Methodist Church Steeple on the right.

The original 13 states had all agreed to turn over their western lands to the United States government when the Articles of Confederation went into effect in March 1781. The U.S. Congress now faced the question of how to govern the public lands west of the Appalachian Mountains. The territory north of the Ohio River offered rich land for settlers. Congress passed the Land Ordinance of 1785, which established a plan for surveying and dividing the land into townships of 36 square miles. Each township would be divided into 36 sections of 1 square mile, or about 640 acres. An individual or family could purchase a section and divide it into farms or smaller units. A typical farm was 160 acres in size.

In 1787, the U.S. Congress further provided for the development of the Northwest Territory by passing the Northwest Ordinance. This ordinance established how states would be created out of the Northwest Territory. And eventually the Northwest Territory became the States of Ohio in 1803, Indiana in 1816, Illinois in 1818, Michigan in 1837, and Wisconsin in 1848.

[It should also be noted that the United States Constitution did not go into effect until 1789, and Rhode Island was the last state to ratify it in 1790.]

But a significant weakness of the Northwest Ordinance of 1787 was that it overlooked the Native American Indians' land claims. And at that time Ohio was a vast wilderness, populated by powerful Indian tribes, that were quite hostile to American settlers. In fact, a confederacy of Indian tribes, including tribes from Ohio, won major victories against the United States in 1790 and 1791. Decisive action had to be taken to protect the young nation's Western Frontier!

For that reason, President George Washington appointed General "Mad" Anthony Wayne, an experienced veteran Revolutionary War leader, to command a new army to subdue the American Indian confederacy. With great enthusiasm, General Wayne accepted his new assignment and began training his new army, as peace negotiations were simultaneously undertaken with the American Indians during the summer of 1793. The United States wanted the territory north of the Ohio River, as agreed upon in the Treaty of Paris of 1783. And American settlers were already moving into Ohio!

Old photograph of Chili looking southwest Road unpaved. Date of photograph unknown.

But two Indian leaders, Shawnee war chief Blue Jacket and Delaware Lenape leader Buckongahelas, encouraged by their recent victories over the United States troops in 1790 and 1791, pressed for the boundary line that had been established with Great Britain in the Treaty of Fort Stanwix in 1768 — long before the Treaty of Paris of 1783. These Native American leaders rejected all treaties that ceded lands north of the Ohio River to the United States.

For this reason, Blue Jacket's army took a strong defensive stand along the Maumee River, where a stand of trees ("fallen timbers") had blown down in a heavy storm. But the American Indians were greatly outnumbered and outflanked by American cavalry. Consequently, the Indian confederacy was decisively defeated at the Battle of Fallen Timbers on August 20th, 1794, and the Native American leaders signed the Treaty of Greenville (1795), giving much of present-day Ohio to the United States.

And once General Wayne had signed the Treaty of Greenville on behalf of the United States, he left Greenville to begin the construction of a line of forts along the Maumee River. Behind this line of forts, Americans settled the Ohio Country, paving the way for Ohio becoming the 17th state in the American union in 1803 — just eight years later!

After Ohio had achieved its statehood, Coshocton County was organized in 1811, although American settlers had been living in the area of Coshocton since 1779. About 1815, a group of Pennsylvania Germans came to Coshocton County and began converting the green wilderness into pleasant hillside farms and villages. Within Coshocton County, New Bedford Village was organized in 1825 and Crawford Township was organized in 1828.

Another old photograph of Chili Village before its roads were paved. Date of picture unknown.

However, it should also be noted that before Crawford Township was officially organized, in the year 1816, Philip and Magdalene Fensler purchased several quarters of military land, in what became Crawford and White Eyes Townships. Later two acres of this land was given by the Fenslers in 1831 to Mount Zion Lutheran Church, to be used for its church and cemetery. The Lutheran church was organized the next year in 1832.

The Fenslers also conveyed several parcels of land to their sons, John and Samuel Fensler, in 1829. On March 10, 1834 these brothers went before John Alexander, a Justice of the Peace, and acknowledged that on March 7, 1834, they had laid out the Town of Chili, and that a surveyor whose name was James Ravenscraft, certified the plot. The surveyor was given the honor of naming the town. He called it Chili, pronounced Chi-li to this very day!

Originally there were 29 lots in the town. Its streets and alleys crossed at right angles. Main Street (now County Road 10) was 60 feet wide; Cross Street was 43 feet wide, and the alleys are each 15 feet wide.

As the population of Chili grew, it supported a post office, several stores (including an I.G.A. Store for about 70 years), the Modern Woodsman Lodge, a telephone office, at least one school, a sawmill, a blacksmith shop, a tannery with a harness and saddle shop, Pete's Inn and Gas Station, a tavern, a print shop, and it had several physicians. Also, Chili was well known for its annual picnic with plenty of food, fun, and friendly social interaction.

I.G.A. Grocery Store in Chili Village. This store was completely destroyed by fire in February 1947.

It should also be noted that although there never was a church right in Chili, there were three churches very close by, and these churches met most of the spiritual needs of the community. As mentioned already Mount Zion Lutheran Church was organized in 1832. Later Chili Methodist Episcopal (German) Church was organized in 1875, and St. John's German Evangelical Church Congregation of Chili, Coshocton County Ohio was organized in 1879. The worship services in all three of these churches were originally conducted in the German language.

Sixty-three families from Germany came to Ohio between 1840 and 1865, and settled in Chili, Baltic, Bakersville, Ragersville, Shanesville, and Fiat. These families came mostly from Rockenhausen and Waldgrehweiler, two communities in Bavaria. It has been said that the hills in Ohio reminded them of the hills back home in Germany.

The 1880 Census indicated that there were 91 people living in Chili. The census also noted that some of these people and their parents were born in Germany.

Chili Village reached its peak population of approximately 400 people in the early 1940's, but its population has since significantly declined. One reason for the decline was that in February, 1947 a huge raging fire of unknown origin destroyed several of its homes and commercial buildings. Another reason was the development of the automobile, which has allowed for greater mobility — especially as the number of automobiles per household has increased.

And as the population of Chili decreased, the local churches were adversely affected. St. John's German Evangelical Church Congregation of Chili closed its doors in 1947, and its building stood unused for several years. Mount Zion Lutheran Church closed in 1969 and Chili Methodist Episcopal (German) Church closed in 1971. All three church buildings were eventually torn down, but the three church cemeteries continue to be well maintained.

CHAPTER 2

The Legacy of St. John's German Evangelical Church Congregation of Chili, Coshocton County, Ohio (1879-1953)

...Christ loved the Church, and gave Himself for it. Ephesians 5.25

In the first chapter of this book three churches were mentioned that met most of the spiritual needs of the people of Chili and the area around it. And although all three of these churches have since closed, one of them, St. John's German Evangelical Church Congregation of Chili, Coshocton County, Ohio, will now be considered in greater detail, because eventually the Chili Crossroads Bible Church acquired its land, building, cemetery, some of its personal property, and a few of its people.

The German Evangelical Protestant St. John's Church of Chile was constructed at a cost of $1,200.00 in 1879, just north of the Village of Chili on a knoll in a grove of Sugar Maple and Hickory trees overlooking the crossroads where County Road 10, County Road 236 and Township Road 88 meet. Because of the unique location of this church building, for decades it has been referred to as "the crossroads church." The United States Geological Society benchmark placed on the church property in 1950 gave the elevation of this location as 846 feet above sea level.

St. John's German Evangelical Church Congregation of Chili at the crossroads before the roads were paved. This church's cornerstone was laid on September 11, 1879.

The church's cornerstone was laid on September 11, 1879. A metal cornerstone box was discovered underneath the church building in 1962. All of the historical records of the original church were in the German language. The box contained a newspaper dated September 1, 1869, a Bible, a church constitution, a church membership roll, the Deutchen Evangelichem Synoge, dated 1877, and a book of catechism which was registered with the United States Congress in 1867.

The church building itself was a large white frame structure, originally having two separate front doors — one for men and the other for women, and a belfry complete with a large church bell. Directly behind the church was its cemetery. The church had at least one exterior door leading outside on its back wall. Also, the church had a small cellar for its coal furnace, which sent heat upstairs through a register in the middle of the floor in the church sanctuary.

St. John's German Evangelical Church Congregation of Chili, Coshocton County, Ohio formally organized in January 1880 with fifteen families. Rev. F. M. Haefelle was its first pastor. A Sunday School was organized several years before in the Chili Schoolhouse and began meeting in the church's building in 1880. There were fifty people enrolled in Sunday School. The church's original members formally held allegiance to the German Reformed Church several miles to the east.

The Trustees of St. John's German Evangelical Church Congregation of Chili, Coshocton County, Ohio received a deed for the church property on July 3rd, 1880 from John and Margaret Lorenz at a cost of $58.00. This deed was recorded in the Coshocton County Clerk's Office on February 2nd, 1882.

St. John's German Evangelical Church Congregation of Chili, Coshocton County, Ohio began keeping its <u>Kirchenbuch</u> (Church Book of Records) on December 1st, 1879. The record keeping was begun by the first pastor, Rev. F.M. Haefelle. The <u>Kirchenbuch</u> was translated into the English language in 1982.

Another photograph of St. John's German Evangelical Church before the roads were paved.

In the church's Kirchenbuch are recorded 166 Baptisms from January 4th, 1880 through November 9th, 1941 performed by five different pastors; 202 Confirmations from April 24th, 1881 through November 21st, 1921 with four pastors mentioned; 23 weddings from June 23rd, 1881 through April 16th, 1940 with two pastors named (five of the weddings took place in the parsonage); 96 deaths are listed in the Death Register from December 1st, 1879 through April 27th, 1941 with five different pastors named. 19 entries in the Death Register are rather long and biographical. The records specifically state that 6 people were buried in cemeteries other than the Crossroads Church Cemetery.

The Village of Chili, a book written by Marjorie A. Wright, privately printed and copyrighted in April 2011, contains an excellent list of the Interments made in the Chili Crossroads Cemetery. This list is in alphabetical order by surnames. Included in this list are 145 interments, with 44 different surnames. Families having the most burials in the cemetery were 16 Lorenzs, 13 Neiss', 10 Heckers, 7 Gregros, and 6 Kleins. Most of the surnames in the cemetery appear to be German in origin. Three of the headstones did not include the deceased's surnames, and three other graves do not have headstones. One deceased person, William Gregro (1921) is listed as removed to Fairfield Cemetery. The oldest grave is that of George Neiss, a four-year-old boy and is dated December 1st, 1879. The most recent grave is that of Eva C. Neiss in 1996. There are no empty graves available in the Chili Crossroads Church Cemetery for additional burials. The Evangelical Congregation of St. John's Church met regularly for approximately sixty-eight years. During these years many changes occurred not only in Chili, but also across America and around the World. Americans experienced Two World Wars, the Great Depression, the Rise and Fall of Nazi Germany, and the Rise of Communism. In addition, most Americans now had electricity in their homes and businesses, telephones, television, and automobiles. Most young people preferred to speak English rather than the native tongue of their parents and grandparents.

And as the population of Chili significantly decreased, the three area churches were adversely affected.

As the Year 1947 closed, the faithful no longer gathered at the church building at the crossroads for worship and fellowship. The church doors remained closed, the lights off, and the beautiful sound of the church's bell could no longer be heard ringing in Chili.

In December 2013, the above monument was placed in the oldest part of the Chili Crossroads Bible Church Cemetery by a descendent of John W. and Margareth (Schlarb) Lorenz, who transferred the original deed to the church and cemetery property to the first church trustees in July 1880. (Please note that both the front and the back of the monument are shown).

CHILI CROSSROADS BIBLE CHURCH CEMETERY
May 2001.

CHAPTER 3

The Reopening of the Old Church at the Crossroads
The Pastorate of Rev. Owen E. Lower
(1953-1961)

*According to the Grace of God which is given unto me, as a wise masterbuilder,
I have laid the foundation, and another buildeth thereon. 1 Corinthians 3:10*

Although the old church at the crossroads remained closed and quiet for approximately five years, God was still working in the hearts and lives of people to accomplish His sovereign purposes and divine will. In fact, the Lord in His wise Providence was preparing a gifted young couple, Rev. and Mrs. Owen and Thelma Lower, to be a blessing to many at home in the United States, as they had been on the foreign mission fields.

Born on July 29th, 1915 at home in Coshocton County, Ohio, Owen E. Lower graduated from Keene High School in 1933, and Wheaton College in Wheaton, IL in 1937. As a young man he received God's Son, the Lord Jesus Christ, as his personal Savior, becoming a born-again Christian. In addition, Owen Lower experienced a call to full-time vocational Christian service. Eventually he married Thelma L. Klassett also born-again Christian, whom he met in college The Lowers served the Lord together as missionaries with the Bible Christian Union in the United States and Europe for many years. The Lowers had no children of their own.

Pastor and Mrs. Owen E. Lower, the church's first pastor and his wife.

But in 1950, Rev. and Mrs. Lower found it necessary to return home to Ohio, after they learned that Owen's parents were both in declining health and needed them. Having returned home, in addition to taking excellent care of Owen's parents, Rev. and Mrs. Owen E. Lower made themselves available for ministry in Ohio. Doors of opportunity opened for Owen to preach locally in churches and over the radio.

In 1951, Rex. Owen E. Lower became the founding pastor of Fresno Bible Church. For several months. this new church met in the home of Myron and Cora Leindecker — right in the town of Fresno. While Pastor Lower was conducting church on the first floor of the Leindecker home, Mrs. Lower would conduct Junior Church in the home's basement. Eventually, a cement block building, which was to be a garage and workshop behind the Leindecker home, was redesigned as the church building and became the church's meeting place for several years. In 1968, Fresno Bible Church purchased land on State Road 93, just South of Fresno, where its beautiful church building is located today.

In 1952, some families in nearby Village of Chili asked Pastor Lower to consider reopening the old closed church at the crossroads. And after giving their request careful prayerful thought, Pastor Lower agreed to serve as pastor of that church, and to continue serving as the pastor of Fresno Bible Church also.

As a result, on March 16th, 1952, the church at the crossroads was reopened, Sunday worship services were held, and a Sunday School was formed with 10 officers and teachers.

On Saturday February 14th, 1953, Pastor Lower began "The Bible Hour," a regular weekly Gospel radio program over Radio Station WTNS in Coshocton, on Saturdays from 11:45 a.m. to Noon, which has been "on the air" ever since. It is the radio station's longest continuously running religious broadcast. And for many years it has been a ministry of Chili Crossroads Bible Church.

A joint meeting of the St. John's German Evangelical Church Congregation of Chili, Coshocton County, Ohio and the Crossroads Bible Church of Chili was called to order on the evening of April 16, 1953. There were fourteen voting members present and minutes of the meeting were taken by Mrs. Thelma E. Lower. The purpose of the meeting was the electing of men to draw up a set of by laws for the new church. Those elected by secret ballot were John Everhart, Edwin Hothem, and Clyde Huprich.

The following quotation is taken from the minutes of that meeting: "After Mr. Lower had called the meeting to order, Harvey Kobel asked for the floor and read the following Resolution: Resolution of transfer of church located at Chili crossroads, Crawford Township, Coshocton County, Ohio. Whereas: The original name of this church is The German Evangelical Protestant St. John's Church of Chili, and as time has passed it has assumed the names of Chili St. John's Evangelical, the German Church of Chili, the Crossroads Church of Chili, etc.; Whereas: this church has been closed for a period of six years for lack of membership and finances, and in want of a minister, Whereas. This church was once denied membership in the Evangelical Synod, Whereas This church has remained a free and independent public institution owned and operated by its membership, which has dwindled to so few members that it is impossible for said members to maintain said church, Whereas: At the request of the public this church be opened as a free and independent, non-denominational church, taking the name of the Chili Crossroads Bible Church, Whereas: The church was re-opened on March 16, 1952, by request of the public, and is flourishing and is self-supporting. Therefore be it resolved: That the old membership of said church approve of the change to a new organization and a new name, known as the Chili Crossroads Bible Church, and be it further Resolved: That the church become the property of the membership of the new organization and that all remaining finances be in the care and jurisdiction of the new officers elected by the new organization."

The Chili Crossroads Bible Church had thirty-one charter members, that included: John Everhart, Mrs. John Everhart, Frank D. Fisher, Mrs. Ruth Fisher, Clarence H. Gregro, Helen Gregro, Mary Haines, Charles Hecker, Edwin Hother, Esther Hothem, Clyde Huprich, Mabel Huprich, Mary Huprich, Valentine Huprich, Harvey Kobel, Miriam Kobel, Owen E. Lower, Thelma K. Lower, Cora McClure, Harry McClure, Theodore]. McQueen, Mrs. Theodore J. McQueen, Henry Mast, Mrs. Henry Mast. Marjorie A. Mathias, Mrs. Mellanie Mathias, Lester R. Miller, Mrs. Lester R. Miller, Lucy Rice, Jim Edward Schlagenhauf, and Amanda Stroup.

Pastor and Mrs. Owen Lower faithfully served both churches for nine years, and regularly and diligently kept the following schedule:

Sundays: 9:30 a.m.	Preaching Service at Chili Crossroads Church
11:00 a.m.	Preaching Service at Fresno Bible Church
7:30 p.m.	Evening Service alternated between the two churches.
Tuesday Evenings:	Bible Class in Newcomerstown
Wednesday Evenings:	Prayer Meeting in Fresno
Thursday Evenings:	Prayer Meeting in Chili
Saturdays: 11:45 a.m.	Live Gospel Broadcast over WTNS

Working along with her dedicated husband, Mrs. Lower was a blessing to both churches — especially in teaching children in Vacation Bible School each summer and in leading the Junior Church Programs. She effectively used her Flannelgraph easel, board, backgrounds, and figures to teach children Bible truths, including the Gospel of Christ.

After pastoring both the Fresno Bible Church and the Chili Crossroads Bible Church for nine years, the Lord led the Lowers to return to their missionary work with the Bible Christian Union in Europe and in the United States. As a couple they then served the Bible Christian Union, until they retired in 1978, when Rev. Owen Lower was approximately 63 years old. After finishing their work with the mission in 1978, the Lowers returned to Coshocton County, and Rev. Lower again served as the Pastor of just the Fresno Bible Church for eight more years from 1978-1986, when he again retired! But still later he served as Interim Pastor of the Chili Crossroads Bible Church from 1987-1988.

Pastor Owen E. Lower died on May 20, 1999 at eighty-three years of age. And approximately five years later, his widow, Mrs. Thelma K. Lower, died on November 28, 2005. Rev. and Mrs. Lower are buried in the Fairfield Cemetery in West Lafayette, Ohio.

CHAPTER 4

Chili Crossroads Bible Church Matures and Becomes Completely Independent
The Pastorate of Rev. James H. Boyd
(1961-1983)

. . . upon this rock I will build My Church, and the Gates of Hell will not prevail against it.
Matthew 16:18

Rev. James H. Boyd accepted the call to be the second pastor of both the Fresno Bible Church and the Chili Crossroads Bible Church in 1961. He was born in Malinta, Ohio on February 13th, 1916, and graduated from high school in Malinta in 1934. As a teenager he had accepted Christ as his own personal Savior, was called to preach at 16 years of age, and was licensed to preach as a high school student. After high school graduation, he enrolled in Moody Bible Institute in Chicago, graduating from Moody in April 1941. While a student at Moody Bible Institute, he served as a student pastor in McClure, Illinois. And at Moody, he met Miss Dorothea Goodrich, who was a student there also. The Boyds were married right after Mrs. Boyd graduated from Moody Bible Institute in August 1941.

Rev. Boyd then continued his education at Wheaton College in nearby Wheaton, Illinois. He pastored several churches, prior to his coming to Fresno and Chili in 1961 with his wife and four children.

For thirteen years from 1961 through the first half of 1974, Rev. Boyd pastored both the Chili Crossroads Bible Church and the Fresno Bible Church. During his pastorate the Fresno church purchased land and built an attractive church building on State Road 93, just south of Fresno.

And meanwhile in Chili, Pastor Boyd and his congregation successfully completed several major projects that enhanced the Chili church. One of these projects was to enlarge the small cellar underneath the church, where the furnace and a small storage area was located, so that there would be a full basement underneath the entire church building. In excavating for this project, workers found old pews and chairs, and also a metal cornerstone box full of records and artifacts which were placed there by the original German congregation. During this time period, new pews were purchased for the church auditorium, and a Service of Dedication for the completed basement project and the new pews was held on November 18th, 1962. Later on, a well was dug and a kitchen and rest rooms were installed in the church basement in 1978. New believers were baptized by immersion in a baptismal tank installed in the church basement. And eventually the outdoor lavatory facilities behind the cemetery were removed.

Background work was also completed, so that the Chili church was incorporated by the State of Ohio on May 1st, 1963.

In October 1970, a new organ was purchased and dedicated.

The refurbishing of the interior of the church auditorium began in January 1973. The ceiling was lowered, new paneling was installed on the inside walls of the church auditorium, and structural work was done so the support pole on the left side of the auditorium could be removed. In addition, a new platform was added. and the floor was carpeted. [The inside of the church had been turned around, so the pulpit was at the back.] Pastor Boyd painted a large Bible Verse Banner that stretched across the front of the church auditorium and read. "Heaven and Earth shall pass away, but My words shall not pass away. (Matthew 24:35)" That banner hung there for the remainder of Rev. Boyd's pastorate at Chili!

The two separate exterior front doors — one for men and the other for women — were removed and a single double door and porch were added to the front of the church. The new entrance doors were painted bright red, as a reminder that the Blood of Jesus Christ, God's only begotten Son, was shed on the Cross of Calvary as full payment for our sins.

On July 5th, 1974 Chili Crossroads Bible Church and Fresno Bible Church became two completely separate churches, and Pastor Boyd became the full-time pastor of just the Chili Crossroads Bible Church. It should be noted that during that time period, the two churches agreed that the weekly Gospel radio broadcast over Station WTNS, begun by Pastor Lower, would continue as a ministry of the Chili Crossroads Bible Church only, and the cost of the broadcast would be fully underwritten by the crossroads church. As previously stated, the broadcast continues to be the oldest religious program on that radio station.

The small cellar underneath the old church was enlarged into a full modern basement, and dedicated in November 1962.

In 1979, Chili Crossroads Bible Church celebrated the 100th Anniversary of its building, and published an anniversary booklet with the title of A Brief History of the Chili Crossroads Bible Church, Chili, Ohio. The 100 Anniversary of the Building 1879-1929. The information in the church's anniversary booklet was compiled by Mrs. Dorthea G. Boyd, Pastor Boyd's wife.

Pastor Boyd concluded his pastorate at Chili Crossroads Bible Church in 1983. His pastorate at Chili Crossroads Bible Church was 22 years in length and is the longest pastorate in the church's history to date. During Pastor Boyd's tenure at Chili, the church became a separate independent church with its own pastor, and improved its building and facilities to allow for a greater ministry in accommodating more people and ministering to them more effectively.

Pastor James H. Boyd died on March 25th, 1987 at 71 years of age. He was survived by his wife, 3 sons, 1 daughter, 3 brothers, 1 sister, and grandchildren.

After Pastor Boyd died, his widow, Mrs. Dorthea G. Boyd, was remarried to another pastor, and lives in Akron, Ohio. She has been most helpful in the preparation of this chapter of this book.

*Pastor and Mrs. James H. Boyd and two of their sons. John and Tim.
Date of photo unknown.*

Chapter 5

The Chili Congregation's Ministry As A Strong Vibrant Bible Church (1983-2004)

For we are laborers together with God; You are God's husbandry,
You are God's Building. I Corinthians 3:9

Pastors Owen Lower and James Boyd were godly men, who diligently served the Lord for more than 30 years as the first two pastors of the Chili Crossroads Bible Church. Through their pastoral leadership, they laid a strong biblical foundation for the church. This next chapter explains that after the completion of these first two pastorates, the Great Lord of the Church sent more godly pastors to Chili, who built upon the strong foundation that was in place.

The Third Pastorate (1983-1987): Rev. Randy Mullins

The church's third pastor was the Reverend Randy Mullins, who was born in Gallipolis, Ohio in August 1955. As a child he received Christ as his personal Savior. Several years later, he graduated from Tri-Valley High School in Dresden, Ohio (1973), and from Bob Jones University in Greenville, South Carolina (1978).

Pastor Mullins, his wife Beth, and their two sons, Joshua and Andrew, came to the Chili Crossroads Bible Church in 1983, and Rev. Mullins served the church faithfully for four years, concluding his ministry at Chili in 1987. As a younger pastor, Reverend Mullins found his ministry in Chili to be quite challenging — especially since his pastorate followed the pastorates of two older and more experienced men. But he served the Lord really well during his tenure at Chili, and later was invited back to the Chili Crossroads Church to fill its pulpit on numerous occasions, over a timespan of several years.

After Pastor Mullins completed his pastorate, Rev. Owen E. Lower was approached by the church's leaders and asked to return to Chili to serve as Interim Pastor of the church. Pastor Lower honored their request, and ministered as Interim Pastor for several months in 1987 and 1988.

The Fourth Pastorate (1988-1999): Rev. Ned Horsfall

The Reverend Ned Horsfall accepted the unanimous call of the Chili Crossroads Bible Church to be its fourth pastor. He began at Chili on June 28, 1988, after serving as pastor of the Faith Baptist Church of Dunbar, Pennsylvania.

Born in Dennison, Ohio on June 8, 1955, Ned Horsfall accepted Jesus Christ as his own personal Savior at a church camp in July 1970. And later he graduated from Indian Valley South High School in Gnadenhutten, Tuscarawas County, Ohio in 1973. After high school graduation, he studied at the Tuscarawas Campus of Kent State University, and then went on to earn a Bachelor of Science Degree at Tennessee Temple University in Chattanooga, TN.

Pastor Ned Horsfall came to the Chili Crossroads Bible Church with his wife, Melissa, who was from the State of Michigan, and their three young children: two sons, JT. and Ryan, and a younger daughter, Emily, who was two years old. Pastor Ned also came to the church with his love for people, an excitement for having the opportunity to minister in his native state of Ohio through the preaching and teaching of the Holy Scriptures, and his strong faith that he would be used by the Holy Spirit of God in the application of God's Word, the Bible, to people's hearts and lives.

As the Reverend Ned Horsfall faithfully pastored the Chili Crossroads Bible Church for more than II years, the church's missionary giving rose from slightly over $200.00 a month to more than $2,000.00 monthly! But in the Fall of 1999 Pastor Horsfall received a call to pastor another Ohio church, and was led of the Lord to conclude his ministry at Chili, in order to accept the call to a new field of service.

The Interim Pastorates of Rev. Daniel C. Meininger and Rev. Daniel M. Kaiser (1999-2001)

After Pastor Horsfall and his family moved on to their next church, Chili Crossroads Bible Church benefited from the ministries of two interim pastors, who served one after the other.

The first of these fine men of God was the Reverend Dan Meininger, who ministered at Chili with his lovely wife, Carolyn, by his side. Pastor Meininger was born in Waverly, Il. on June 24th, 1941. His grandfather and his father were also ordained ministers before him. Pastor Dan served as Interim Pastor through December 2000, but assisted the Chili church on many occasions after that. Reverend Meininger often said to his wife that his time at Chili was one of his most rewarding experiences in his life. He loved the people and enjoyed teaching them. He would tell his wife, Carolyn, that they were so hungry for the Word of God!

After serving as Interim Pastor of the Chili Crossroads Bible Church, Reverend Meininger continued to be a blessing and a wise counselor to the Chili Church — up to the very time that he was promoted to Heaven on September 9th, 2007 — two days after he had participated in the groundbreaking service for the building of a brand-new church building at Chili crossroads (*see Chapter 6*).

Pastor Daniel and Carolyn Meininger outside the front entrance of the original church building.

Rev. Daniel M. Kaiser began his interim pastorate at Chili on the first Sunday of January 2001. At that time, he was and still is a church-planting missionary in Trieste, Italy, serving with the Evangelical Alliance Mission of Wheaton, Illinois. Born in Brooklyn, New York on May 27th, 1956, Dan trusted in Christ as Savior after searching for the true way of salvation, and turning to the Bible, which became for him the reliable source he needed for discovering that Jesus Christ is the Way, the Truth, and the Life, and that no one comes to the Heavenly Father except through Him (John 14:6). He graduated from Brick Town High School in New Jersey, spent three years serving in the United States Army, and later attended Grand Rapids School of the Bible and Music in Michigan, and later graduated from Grace Bible College in 1985.

When Reverend Kaiser came to Chili as Interim Pastor, he brought with him his beautiful wife, Suzanne, and his three young daughters Sabrina, Sarah, and Claire. And at the church, he taught the Adult Sunday School Class, preached both morning and evening on Sundays, conducted the weekly prayer services, spoke on the weekly radio broadcast, and made pastoral visits. He concluded his ministry just before the Year 2001 ended, when the next regular pastor arrived, and the Kaisers then began final preparations for their return to foreign missionary service in Italy.

It should be noted that the Chili Crossroads Bible Church continues to regularly pray for the Kaisers, and has included them in its missionary budget. And when home on furlough, the Kaisers visit the church to share with the Chili congregation the blessings and prayer requests associated with their missionary ministry to the Italian people.

The Fifth Pastorate: Rev. David C. Macy (2001-2004)

The fifth pastor of the Chili Crossroads Bible Church was the Reverend David C. Macy.

Born in Bridgeport, Connecticut in June 1945, David Macy accepted Christ as personal Savior at a youth rally in Philadelphia, Pennsylvania in November 1961. A couple of years later he graduated from South Philadelphia High School in 1963, from Philadelphia College of Bible in 1968, and from Talbot Theological Seminary with two theological degrees in 1971 and 1973. He also earned a Diploma in French. He and his wife, Lois, are the parents of two grown sons.

Before coming to Chili, Reverend Macy pastored a church in Bagdad, Arizona, and also taught in the Arizona College of the Bible from 1977-1988. One of his students at the college was Chris Cutshall, who grew up near West Lafayette, Ohio and was a member of Fresno Bible Church. Later on, in 1986, Mr. Cutshall returned to Ohio to become the Pastor of Fresno Bible Church. In his capacity as pastor of the Fresno church, the Lord allowed Pastor Cutshall to introduce Pastor Macy to the Chili church, which resulted in David Macy becoming the next regular pastor of the Chili church. Pastor Macy said later, "Ohio is one of the most beautiful areas we have been in!"

On June 2nd, 2002, the Coshocton Tribune published an attractive article on its front page with pictures, which continued on page 3A: "Rural Church Thrives. Despite Tiny Population, Church in Chili Fills Its Pews." This newspaper article, written about the Chili Crossroads Bible Church, continued by saying that the church has many parishioners and fills its pews on Sundays. Pastor Macy is quoted saying, "Many people are attracted to our ministry."

Pastor Macy concluded his Chili pastorate in 2004, in order to move to Springfield, Ohio to serve the Lord in a chaplaincy ministry, linked to the family medical practice belonging to his two sons, Dr. Joel D. Macy and Dr. Kevin P. Macy.

Chapter Summary:

Pastors Mullins, Horsfall, Meininger, Kaiser, and Macy all faithfully preached the Gospel, taught the Bible, ministered to the people, and promoted home and foreign missions in the church and over the radio, and in so doing, built on the strong biblical foundation that the first two pastors of the church had laid, and as a result the Chili Crossroads Bible Church moved ahead into the 21st Century as a strong vibrant Bible Church for the Glory of God.

Chapter 6

The LORD'S Great Answers to Sincere Prayer at Chili (2004-2009)

Let us therefore come boldly unto the Throne of Grace, that we may obtain mercy, and find grace to help in time of need. Hebrews 4:16

After Pastor David Macy concluded his ministry at the Chili Crossroads Bible Church, the church's leadership was not able to immediately find a permanent replacement for him. As a result, Mr. John D. Kandel served as Interim Student Pastor from Sunday July 4th, 2004 thru Easter Sunday April 12th, 2009 — a period of approximately four and one-half years. Brother John Kandel and his wife Beth came to Chili when he was 27 years old. A 1996 Graduate of Hiland High School in Berlin, Ohio, John Kandel served in the United States Marine Corps from 1997 thru 2001. Later he enrolled as a student at an Ohio extension campus of Moody Bible Institute, and served the Chili church as Interim Student Pastor. He was never licensed or ordained, but he was encouraged and mentored by the Reverend Daniel C. Meininger, already mentioned in this book. It should be noted that Brother Kandel did a good job "filling the gap" when no one else was available. Brother Kandel was and is a strong people-person with a heart for the Lord and for ministry.

In January 2006 — about a year and a half after the Kandels came to Chili — a core group of Chili believers began to faithfully meet on Sunday evenings before the evening services to pray specifically for the spiritual welfare of the church, for God's direction for the church, and for a full-time senior pastor. Soon the attendees of those Sunday Prayer Meetings were convinced that the Lord heard and answered their sincere prayers. As the Chili people regularly and faithfully prayed for their church, the Lord answered their prayers — much differently than in the ways they had anticipated!

In April 2006, some unusual noises were heard above the ceiling of the Chili church sanctuary. A competent carpenter was sent up into the church attic to investigate, but he found nothing wrong up there.

And yet, on Thursday May 4th, 2006 a main support beam collapsed in the old church, resulting in the church building's total destruction. On that day, members of one of the church's families, Rick Glazer and his two daughters, were cutting the grass around the church. One of his daughters went into the church to get a cold drink of water and came out a moment later. All three of them then heard a loud cracking sound. and when they went to open the church door, debris came out and filled the door space! They quickly stepped away as an avalanche of debris and dust came out the door — and made its way all the way out to the road! Thankfully, by the Grace of God, no one was hurt!

Eventually the old church had to be professionally demolished in December 2006. The large old church bell was salvaged and has been retained by the church. But the stately old church building was reduced to rubble and had to be carted away. The Chili Crossroads Bible Church found a temporary meeting place, first in a local banquet hall on County Road 236, and later in the Fresno Public School.

Where was the church to go? What was the church to do? The church's leadership soon realized that old church property with its cemetery was not large enough to allow for the building of a new church building on the same parcel of land. Modern construction codes could not be met with the amount of land the church already owned. The church needed more land! And the Sunday evening prayer warriors added to their list of specific prayer requests, a request for an appropriate larger parcel of land on which to build a new church building!

This large old church bell was rescued from the ruins, when the old church was demolished.

It should be noted that across County Road 10 from the old church and cemetery was a large field belonging to an Amish farm owned by Robert M. and Anna Mae Troyer. The Chili church leaders believed that the front portion of that field would be the ideal place for the new church to be built — just across County Road 10 from the old church property. But when Mr. Troyer was approached, he was not interested in selling his farm land to the church — or to anyone else for that matter. And four other land owners in the general area of the old church also declined to sell their land to the church. But still the Sunday evening prayer group persisted in praying in faith-believing for appropriate land on which to build their new church building! Indeed, all summer long the church prayed for land! But the 2006-2007 School Year started, and the church had no idea where they would build their new church. But the people still faithfully and earnestly prayed for land, and also for a senior pastor for the Chili Crossroads Bible Church.

On Monday October 2nd, 2006, a terrible tragedy occurred in a rural area of Lancaster County, Pennsylvania which made the national news. By 8:00 a.m., that morning, twenty-six children ages 6 to 13 from ten nearby Amish homes arrived at the West Nickel Mines School as usual. Their twenty-year-old teacher, Emma, called school to order, and then welcomed four special ladies to school, including her own mother, who were visiting that morning. She then read the Bible and led the class in reciting the Lord's Prayer. After that, she had the class sing three songs which spoke of their Christian faith. Emma then began her teaching for the day.

About 10:15 a.m... that morning, a thirty-two-year-old man, Charles Carl Roberts, IV, entered the schoolhouse, waved a gun, and ordered everyone to lie down on the floor in the front of the classroom. Seeing the gun and knowing that other adults were in the room, Emma, the young teacher, and her mother ran nearly a quarter of a mile across the fields for help. In the meantime, Roberts ordered the three other visitors and the eleven boys to leave. Roberts planned to kill all of the girls immediately! Thankfully one of the school girls escaped. But five others were shot to death, and the other five were critically injured by the gunfire, and then struggled for their very lives.

This great tragedy impacted not only the Amish homes from which the children came, but Amish and English people everywhere, including the large Amish population in Ohio. News of the Nickel Mines massacre spread quickly across the nation and around the world. And Amish people everywhere, including those who resided in Coshocton County, Ohio mourned not only the loss of the Pennsylvania Amish school girls, but the loss of Charles Roberts' life as well, and earnestly prayed for the healing of the ones who were injured.

Two days later on Wednesday October 4th, the Chairman of the Board of the Chili Crossroads Bible Church, Brother Mike Ianniello, was approached by Henry M. Troyer, his near Amish neighbor on County Road 236 Henry told Mike that Robert M. Troyer, the Amish farmer on County Road 10, wanted to see him. And when they met, Robert Troyer told him that the school shooting in Pennsylvania had so badly upset him that he couldn't sleep, and in the night, he had decided that he would sell some of his land to the Chili Crossroads Bible Church!

An informal agreement was soon reached between Mr. and Mrs. Robert Troyer and the Board of the Chili Crossroads Bible Church. Afterwards Mr. Troyer reported that he was at peace, after agreeing to this land sale, and it has been learned that his Amish neighbors were hoping that he would sell his land to the church. A little over two acres of land along County Road 10, for the more-than-fair price of $15,000.00, was purchased by the church. This land was surveyed in November 2006 and certified on the 27th of that month as containing 2.4722 Acres with 176.29 feet of frontage along the west side of County Road 10 — diagonally across from the original church and cemetery. In March 2007, the church received A General Warranty Deed for its new property, which had been recorded in the Recorders Office of Coshocton County.

As the Congregation of the Chili Crossroads Bible Church praised the Lord for the additional land on which to erect its new church, the church's board lost no time in engaging an Architect to prepare plans for the new church. Once these plans were accepted, the next step was to name Robert Miller of the Ohio Dutch Construction Company of Millersburg. Ohio as the General Contractor for the building of the new church. A Groundbreaking Service was held on Sunday Afternoon September 9th, 2007, and construction began a short time later.

Pastor Dan Meininger reads from his Bible at the Groundbreaking Service for the new church.

The construction workers were able to work all through the Fall months in 2007, and throughout the Winter of 2007-2008, making it possible for the Church to be able to have its First Service in its Pastor Dan Meininger reads from his Bible at the Groundbreaking Service for the new church. new church building on April 20th, 2008, and an Open House for the brand-new building a little less than a month later on May 18th, 2008!

The new church building was absolutely beautiful! It has an attractive Foyer with halls leading to the various rooms, a beautifully carpeted sanctuary with high ceilings and the windows up near the ceiling, a large platform, with a lighted cross, a baptistry in the floor, and choir rooms on each side of the platform. In the rear of the sanctuary is an elevated sound system platform with a professional audio control board. The new building also has a small Fellowship Hall, a Serving Kitchen, an office for the Pastor, a Nursery with its own lavatory, and two modern Rest Rooms. The building is complete with central air conditioning and heating, a vehicular entranceway, and a beautiful steeple.

It should be mentioned that a three-phase 240-volt electrical service was required for the church's air conditioning and heating system to function properly. And as plans were being made for construction of the new church, it was discovered that the local electric company had run three-phase service right to the edge of the new church property before the church had even purchased the land. The required electrical service was in place for the church without additional expense to the church!

Beautiful chimes are regularly played inside and outside the church before the services. And the new church and the land it sits on are completely paid for! The Lord wonderfully answered prayer for more land and a new church building.

And as the prayer warriors thanked the Lord for the provision of a church, and the land on which it was built, they continued to earnestly pray for a permanent full-time senior pastor. And the need seemed to become even more urgent when the congregation learned that their Student Interim Pastor, John Kandel and his wife, Beth, felt that it was time for them to move on. And Easter Sunday, April 12th, 2009 was their last Sunday at the Chili Crossroads Bible Church.

"But my God shall supply all your need according in glory by Christ Jesus." Philippians 4:19

A large sign was erected to show where the new church building would be located.

Pastor John Kandle and Brother Mike Ianiello prepare to break ground for the new church. Board members Mike Miller and Jim Priest watch.

The walls of the new church building could soon be seen from County Road 10.

The shingles being installed on the lower roof of the new church building.

A rear view of the new church building.

The new church sanctuary nearing completion.

Chili Crossroads Bible Church's attractive new steeple.

The above photo was taken before the old church collapsed in 2007.

The Open House for the new church building was held on May 18, 2008.

CHAPTER 7

The Preparatory Ministry of Pastor Joseph Essington (Spring - Summer - Fall, 2009)

And the things that thou hast heard of me among many witnesses, the same commit thou to faithful men, who shall be able to teach others also. II Timothy 2:2

Reverend David J. Bauer of Bible Related Ministries, Inc., located near Chicago, Illinois, gave Mike and Brenda Ianniello the name of Pastor Joseph Essington in New Jersey. Rev. Bauer said that Brother Essington might be available to help their church in Ohio, and he followed up his suggestion by sending them Pastor Essington's Information Sheet.

Pastor Joseph Essington was born on February 7th, 1941 in Swedesboro, Gloucester County in Southern New Jersey. When he was an eighth-grade student, a Christian family took him with them to Gospel meetings in the Park Bible Baptist Church of Pennsville, New Jersey, where he clearly heard and understood for the first time the Gospel of Christ. A short time later, he heard the Bible Verse, John 3:16, and as a result he believed on the Lord Jesus Christ as his own personal Savior and became a child of God. Later on, as a high school student, he experienced a Call to Preach, and began preaching the Gospel during his Junior Year of high school. As a school senior he was licensed to preach, a few weeks before he graduated from Penns Grove Regional High School in New Jersey in June 1959 and was ordained in 1965. Later he graduated from Shelton College (NJ) in 1965 and Grace Theological Seminary in 1979.

Dr. A. Joseph Essington, known to many as "Pastor Joe" or "Brother Joe" is also a graduate of the American Correctional Chaplaincy Training School. Later he received a Doctor of Letters Degree in 2003. In addition to being an ordained pastor and chaplain; he is also a New Jersey certified teacher. Dr. Essington served as the Chaplain of the McAuley Water Street Mission in New York City, as a teacher and administrator in Christian schools for more than 20 years, and as the Senior Chaplain and Director of Inmate Services of the Salem County Correctional Facility (NJ). Dr. Essington and his wife, Barbara, have been married for over forty years, and they have four adult children and four grandchildren.

In March 2009, Mike Ianniello called Pastor Joe in New Jersey, and Joe Essington agreed to visit the church in Ohio with his wife, Barbara, during her Easter Recess from school. [As previously mentioned, Easter Sunday April 12th was to be John and Beth Kandel's last Sunday.] On Wednesday April 15th, the Essingtons visited Chili for the first time. They spent most of the day with Mike and Brenda, were given a tour of most of Coshocton County, observed the church's Annual Business Meeting that night, and at the end of the meeting Pastor Joe spoke briefly to the congregation. After that meeting, Mike took him to Radio Station WTNS in

Coshocton, so that Pastor Essington could record a message for the church's weekly radio broadcast. It was a very *long* day!

The Chili church wanted the Essingtons to come and help them right away. But Pastor and Mrs. Essington needed some time to be sure that it was the Lord's Will. That Saturday, April 18th, Pastor Joe called Mike and told him that he would definitely come to Chili and stay for as long as the church needed him. But before he could leave New Jersey, he had to complete some speaking engagements, and he had an important doctor's appointment. On Saturday May 9th, Pastor Joe called Mike again, and said that he had received a good report from the doctor, and he would be coming to Ohio on Thursday May 21st. His wife, Barbara, would follow him when the school year was complete.

Pastor Joe drove to Ohio on Thursday the 21st. He stayed temporarily in the Comfort Inn in Dover, Ohio. Later, arrangements were made by the church for the Essingtons to occupy the beautiful Missionary Apartment belonging to the Dale and Deborah Coates family not far from Coshocton. The Coates are home missionaries with MMS Aviation, a missionary agency which prepares People and Planes for World Missionary Service. Dale and Deborah Coates, and their daughters Kirsty and Ruth-Anne, and the Essingtons enjoyed many good times of fellowship together and have become good friends! And it should be noted that Chili Crossroads Bible Church has prayerfully and financially supported the missionary endeavors of MMS Aviation for many years.

Pastor Essington's first Sunday with the Chili church was the day before Memorial Day, Sunday May 24th, 2009, when he preached on "A Memorial Forever!" from Joshua 4:1-7. That weekend he spent time fellowshipping with the church people. The next week he got right to work. Beginning on Tuesday, he was in his church office every morning, he made a pastoral visit in Baltic on Wednesday, he led Prayer Meeting on Wednesday evening, was present for the church's Board meeting on Thursday evening, and made a Hospital Call in Canton on Friday. The following Tuesday he went to Radio Station WTNS and recorded the next two weekly Gospel radio broadcasts. On his first visit to the radio station, he made a standing appointment to record two more Gospel broadcasts every other Tuesday morning.

Pastor Joseph Essington standing in the pulpit of the Chili Crossroads Bible Church Summer 2009.

As Pastor Essington carefully prepared his radio messages and faithfully went to the radio station for his recording sessions, he was reminded of his late friend and employer at Sandy Cove Bible Conference near North East, Maryland, back when he was a Junior and Senior in high school. Pastor George A. Palmer, the Director of the conference, always ended his daily radio broadcasts by saying, "And Remember Friends, JESUS NEVER FAILS!" He also recalled that Sandy Cove soloist, Carol Sue Perkins, would open and close those broadcasts by singing, "Jesus Never Fails" The Lord used those fond memories to lead Pastor Essington to obtain a sound track of "Jesus Never Fails" for the radio broadcasts, and he consistently ended each broadcast with the words, "And Remember Friends, JESUS NEVER FAILS!"

Almost every day, except Sundays, Pastor Essington went to the Fresno Post Office to pick up the church's mail and his personal mail. Then he would go to the church. During his first weeks at Chili, he organized the Pastor's Office *which really had not been used before*. Someone donated a good desk, another person gave a bookcase, a file cabinet belonging to the church was located, and the church was given a computer. The people saw the pastor's car every morning at the church, and some of them stopped in to talk, and others called him on the phone. Every other Wednesday that summer, the Coshocton County Bookmobile came to the Chili church parking lot, so that the local children and adults could borrow and return library books. Pastor Essington made it his practice to visit the bookmobile and warmly greet the children and adults who used the library, and also the library staff. Most afternoons after lunch, he visited in the homes of church members and prospects.

Pastor Joseph Essington teaching the Adult Sunday School Class at Chili Crossroads Bible Church. Summer 2009.

Pastor Essington did take a day off each week, either on Thursday or Friday. But early on Saturday morning he and his wife, Barbara, would set up our Table at the Fresno Farmers Market, and offer people free Bibles, tracts, church literature, and cold bottled water. He also prepared an Album of Pictures of Chili Crossroads Bible Church, which he used at the market to explain the history and ministries of the church and its Gospel Radio Broadcasts. Many friendships were made at the weekly farmer's market.

Mrs. Barbara Essington at the church's display table. Fresno Farmer's Market. Summer 2009.

Generally speaking, an Interim Pastor is considered a "temporary shepherd," who serves the local church by preaching and teaching the Word of God, and by providing pastoral leadership and pastoral counseling while the church is between permanent pastors. Usually, it is understood that the Interim Pastor will not become the next permanent pastor, nor will he become involved in the selection process of choosing the next pastor. Pastor Essington kept these considerations in mind as he ministered at the Chili Crossroads Bible Church.

However, soon after his coming to Ohio, the Board of Directors of Chili church asked Essington to become involved by giving him copies of some resumes of potential pastors that the board had been considering. One of the resumes he received was that of a young ordained preacher, whose name is Rev. Neal Dearyan. Brother Neal and his family lived in Wauconda, Illinois and he and his wife both were on staff at the Quentin Road Bible Baptist Church in Lake Zurich, Illinois.

Later the Chairman of the church's Board of Directors asked Pastor Joe if he himself would consider becoming the next permanent pastor. Pastor Joe emphatically said, "No," and went on to explain that he felt that he was too old to be the long-term pastor that the church really needed for the church to grow and thrive. In the same conversation, Pastor Joe got out his copy of Rev. Neal Dearyan's resume, and said that Neal was in the right age bracket to serve as their next regular pastor. Pastor Essington went on to say that it was his candid opinion that the other resumes that he had been given were for men who were "too old" also.

Pastor Essington then learned that Neal Dearyan had spoken one Sunday at Chili before he started his ministry in Ohio. He suggested that Rev. and Mrs. Neal Dearyan be invited back to Chili, so that the church could hear him preach again, and have the opportunity to talk again with Neal and his wife. He also said that during their visit, he would be willing to interview Neal and Julie Dearyan himself, and give an opinion to the church's leadership as to whether or not he thought that the Dearyans would be a "good fit" for the Chili church.

In keeping with Dr. Essington's suggestion, Rev. and Mrs. Neal Dearyan and their two children returned to Chili the weekend of July 13th and 14th. Pastor Neal preached both morning and evening that Lord's Day, and Pastor Essington spent some quality time with the Dearyans the day before. Pastor and Mrs. Dearyan were asked to visit the Adult Sunday School Class, so that the Chili people would have the opportunity to become better acquainted with the couple, and ask them any questions about their current ministry and their goals for future ministry. The Chili people really liked the Dearyans, and began to seriously pray about the possibility of Brother Neal Dearyan becoming their next full-time permanent pastor. After the Dearyans had gone home, the members of the Chili Crossroads Bible Church were polled, and expressed a strong interest in extending a pastoral call to Rev. Neal and Julie Dearyan.

The church congregation was given proper notice that there would be a Special Congregational Meeting on Sunday July 5th for the purpose of voting whether or not to extend a Pastoral Call to Rev. Neal Dearyan. And when that congregational meeting was held, the church voted unanimously to extend a Call to Pastor Neal Dearyan. There were no negative votes and no abstentions. And a few days later the Chili congregation learned that the Dearyans had accepted the Pastoral Call and would arrive in Chili on or about September 1st! It was agreed that the church would rent a home for them to live in near Chili, since the church did not own a parsonage, and it would take some time for Pastor Neal and Julie to sell the home they owned in Illinois.

In order that there would be a smooth transition, and because this would be Pastor Neal's first senior pastorate, the Essingtons agreed to remain in Ohio through the end of September, and help the Dearyans get started in their new ministry.

Most of the Dearyans' belongings arrived at their Chili home by truck before Labor Day, and Pastor Neal and Julie and their children arrived with their fully-loaded cars shortly afterwards. When the couple and their children arrived at their new home, located about ¼ mile South of the church on County Road 10, they discovered that someone had set up a large-lighted and very visible Buck Eyes Mascot Display on their front lawn! The Chili church people had not only cleaned their new house, but had filled the refrigerator and pantry with an abundant supply of food, including some delicious meals *prepared by the church ladies*!

The Dearyan family lost no time in arranging their furniture, unpacking their suitcases, and opening and emptying their many cartons of possessions.

Pastor Essington preached at Chili on Sunday morning September 6th, and invited Pastor Neal to lead the second half of the Communion Service. The next Sunday was Installation Sunday. Dr. James A. Scudder, the Senior Pastor of Quentin Road Bible Baptist Church, preached in the morning service, and the Installation Service for Pastor Neal Dearyan was held that afternoon. Several guest pastors were given a part in that service and many church people and visitors were present for the Installation Service. Pastor Essington presided at the service and offered the Prayer of Installation. When the service concluded, almost everyone stayed for the delicious Installation Dinner.

The following Sunday, September 20th, Pastor Neal began his preaching ministry in his new church. And Pastor Joe spent the rest of the month in making suggestions, showing Pastor Neal where the church people lived, and getting him started with the radio ministry. He also bought Pastor Neal a few more professional books for his library.

A Farewell Service for the Essingtons was held on Sunday evening September 27th, and both Pastor Joe and Barbara spoke to the congregation that evening. On Wednesday September 30th the Essingtons drove both of their cars back to New Jersey, with their pet part-Siamese cat, La-La, who had made two trips from New Jersey to Ohio with Barbara. The Essingtons continue to pray regularly for the Chili church, and they have returned several times to encourage the Chili folks — especially the ones in the congregation who were facing great difficulties. Pastor Essington wrote this history of the Chili Crossroads Bible Church because of his love for the church and its congregation.

Therefore, my beloved brethren, be ye steadfast, unmovable,
always abounding in the Work of the LORD.
Forasmuch as ye know that your labor is not in vain in the LORD. I Corinthians 15.58
Pastor Joe's Life Bible Verse

Pastor Joe and Barbara Essing, while visiting the First Bags Church of Cape May, NJ in September 2010.

Pastor Neal explaining a display in the lobby of the Quentin Road Bible Baptist Church. August 26th, 2009.

CHILI CROSSROADS BIBLE CHURCH
SERVICE OF INSTALLATION
of Brother Neal Dearyan as Senior Pastor
Dr. Joseph Essington, Interim Pastor Presiding

Prelude

Words of Welcome and Greeting

Hymn #131	"The Church's One Foundation"
Invocation	Pastor David Kraft First Baptist Church, West Lafayette
Scripture Reading	Pastor David Fowls Perry Chapel Baptist Church, Warsaw
Challenge to the Church	Dr. James A. Scudder Quentin Road Bible Baptist Church, Chicago
Challenge to the Pastor	Pastor David J. Bauer Bible Related Ministries
Prayer of Installation	Pastor Joseph Essington
Acceptance of the Pastorate	Brother Neal Dearyan
Hymn #449	"Take My Life and Let It Be"
Benediction	Pastor Neal Dearyan

Postlude

Installation Service Program.

*Installation Service for Pastor Neal Dearyan on September 13th, 2009.
Dr. Joseph Essington presiding.*

Chapter 8

An Active Growing Church with a Vision for the Future
The Ongoing Ministry of Pastor Neal and Julie Dearyan
(2009-Present)

Where there is no vision, the people perish. Proverbs 29:18

Enlarge the place of thy tent, and let them stretch forth the curtains of thy habitation: spare mot, lengthen thy cords, and strengthen thy stakes. Isaiah 54:2

When October 2009 arrived, the Essingtons were back in New Jersey, new signs of Fall were seen daily everywhere in Ohio, and Pastor Neal and Julie Dearyan were developing their new ministry at Chili with great enthusiasm and earnest dedication. As a pastoral couple they were very friendly and outgoing, and brought many well-tested and proven ideas to Ohio with them from the Quentin Road Bible Baptist Church, where they had both been on staff!

Rev. Neal Dearyan was born on August 18th, 1972 in California. He was raised and homeschooled in a Christian home near Hot Springs, Arkansas. As a child, he trusted Jesus Christ as his personal Savior, while listening to the Gospel of John being read. Soon he clearly confessed the Lord Jesus Christ as his personal Savior, and then he obediently followed the Lord in the waters of Believer's Baptism at only eight years of age.

As he grew up, Pastor Neal worked in his father's land surveying business from 1987 through 1991, and trained to be a boundary topographical surveyor, and prepared to be certified as a professional land surveyor in Arkansas. But the Lord had other plans for him. At age 17, he had the opportunity to attend a church camp in Minnesota. At that camp he learned about Dayspring Bible College, a ministry of the Quentin Road Bible Baptist Church in Lake Zurich, Illinois.

Neal visited the college, and in so doing, he became better acquainted with the Quentin Road Bible Baptist Church. He became convinced that Lake Zurich was where the Lord really wanted him to be! And the Lord opened the doors for him to not only study at Dayspring Bible College, but also to work in the various ministries of the Quentin Road Baptist Church for some eighteen years!

This attractive new sign was installed soon after Pastor Neal came in 2009.

While at the church, the Lord blessed Neal Dearyan in many different ways. And one of those ways was that he became acquainted with Miss Julie Ann Scudder, the pastor's only daughter, who was also a church staff member! Eventually Neal and Julie began dating, later became engaged, and were married on May 7th, 1993. And now Pastor and Mrs. Dearyan are the proud parents of two great teenagers, James and Amanda.

In May 2000, Neal graduated from Dayspring Bible College, having earned a Bachelor of Arts Degree — *both in Bible Studies and Pastoral Studies*. He then pursued graduate studies at Dayspring Seminary on a part-time basis, and received his Master's Degree from Dayspring University in 2009.

From 1992 to 2009, Neal had served as an Assistant Pastor at Quentin Road Bible Baptist Church, and in that capacity was the Director of Ministries for the church's *Victory in Grace* Radio and Television Ministries. His wife, Julie, an excellent writer, worked right along with him by serving as the Editor of the *Victory in Grace Magazine*, and as the Co-host of the Victory in Grace Radio and TV Ministries.

Soon after beginning his new ministry at Chili, Pastor Neal was asked about his goals for his new ministry in Ohio. He replied, "My vision for Chili is to teach the Word of God and to love the people. As I do these two things, we can all look to God to work through us to reach our community for Christ."

One of the first tasks that Pastor Neal accomplished for the church was to develop a beautiful interactive website. It includes beautiful photographs of church activities, past and current sermons and radio broadcasts, various links, Pastor Neal's Blog, and church news and announcements. Currently the church's website is being visited on an average of 1000 times monthly. Readers will find this website at www.chilibiblechurch.org/.

In his early days in Ohio, Pastor Neal also tackled some other needed work. An attractive illuminated sign was installed in front of the church on County Road 10. This large sign includes both permanent wording and space for removable lettering and symbols that can be changed to advertise the seasonal events of the church and its ministries. Also, a locking mailbox was installed outside the church along the road, and as a result the church's post office box at the Fresno Post Office was eliminated.

By Thanksgiving 2009, Julie Dearyan had organized a church choir, a Kids Club on Wednesday evenings, a Children's Church Program, and she was guiding the church's young people into Christian drama activities. In the 2009, Thanksgiving Service was special music rendered by the choir and a drama presentation given by the teens. The choir soon had risers to stand on when they sang!

On Christmas Sunday December 20th, 2009, the Kids Club, gave a magnificent performance before an audience of over 70 people. And more than 80 people attended the church's Christmas Eve Service on December 24th.

About a year after the Dearyans arrived, the church began purchasing more radio time to broadcast their weekly radio program on a second radio station — in effect doubling the potential listening audience. Pastor Essington's custom of concluding each broadcast with the reminder, "Jesus Never Fails!" and playing the hymn, "Jesus Never Fails" is being continued on the broadcasts. (The original broadcast was started by the first pastor of the church, Rev. Owen E. Lower).

As the church expands its ministries, and as Pastor Neal and Julie and their children have become better known, more and more people are visiting the Chili church, liking what they are finding there, and attending on a regular basis. And as the church's attendees have grown, a number of adjustments have been made to accommodate the additional people. The church's pews have been put into storage, so that the larger numbers of people might be comfortably seated on the attractive 250 portable stacking cushioned chairs that the church has acquired. The rooms on either side of the platform in the church sanctuary have been cleaned out to be used as classroom space. The new Projection Screens on the upper front walls of the church sanctuary are used in most of the services. Quite a while ago, a modern 33 passenger bus was purchased to transport children and young people to and from church, and also to take people on meaningful church outings.

This writer has observed that Pastor Neal and Julie possess good parenting skills. Their attractive home is safe refuge and a happy haven, not only for their two teenagers, but for other young people as well. And Pastor and Julie have good rapport with the parents living in Chili and surrounding areas.

A significant number of people have accepted the Lord Jesus Christ as personal Savior under Pastor Neal's ministry. And, at the time that this is being written, 31 people have been scripturally baptized in the church's Baptistry, and at least 45 people have been received as new members of the Chili church. And there are a few more who want to be baptized and some who want to join the church at the present time. The Baptistry in the new church had never been used prior Pastor Neal coming to the church.

Pastor Neal has enthusiastically promoted the Chili church's burden of supporting home and foreign missions. The church continues to have its Annual Missionary Conference each year. And in addition, as its Thanksgiving Project in November 2010, the church collected food and other supplies for the Haven of Rest Mission in Akron, Ohio. More recently, the Chili young people visited the Akron mission for a day, doing volunteer work around the facility.

As this book is about to go to press, the Dearyans have been at Chili Crossroads Bible Church five years. And their ministry is still growing and gaining momentum! The church's thriving "Kids Ministry" continues on Wednesday evenings. On a recent Wednesday evening, the closing AWANA Program and Awards Night was held. Before the program began, delicious Pizza was served to all who wanted it on a freewill donation basis. In the front of the auditorium, the projection screens flashed "2012 was an Awesome Year at Chili!" Next, they said "2013 is going to be even Awesomer!" Approximately 100 children and young people were present for the program. Each AWANA group participated. Substantial prizes were awarded to the young people for their achievements. As the program concluded, Pastor Neal gave a clear Gospel message. After the program ended, a 100 Foot Banana Split was served to the AWANA participants in a nearby room.

And when the AWANA Program concludes until September each year, there are numerous other activities for the Spring and Summer months, including PIZZA being served every Wednesday night, the IGNITE Summer Youth group every Wednesday, TALKTIME, a one-on-one Discipleship Ministry for Adults meeting throughout the Summer, and the FORT RAPIDS PARK TRIP, the CEDAR POINT TRIP, the CHILI FAMILY FAIR, the FAMILY AND TEEN CAMP and the GRACE CONFERENCE held near Chicago!

In addition to all of the above planned activities, the church has recently installed a 50 by 50-foot well-equipped Playground on its church property, and has acquired a second bus (14 Passenger) to assist in transporting people to and from church activities. The church is also serving as the home base for a Home School Co-Op, which currently includes four families, and has the potential to grow substantially larger.

It is abundantly clear to this writer that Pastor Neal and Julie Dearyan are a gifted young pastoral couple, who with their children have been providentially led to the Chili Crossroads Bible Church for the glory of God — to be a blessing to the church and its people, and to those outside of the church who will benefit from hearing and believing the Gospel of our Lord Jesus Christ. And as the final chapter of this book is closing, our wonderful LORD continues to bless His Church at Chili and the ministry of Pastor Neal and Julie Dearyan.

TO GOD BE THE GLORY!

"God's Work done in God's, will never lack God's Supply."
—Hudson Taylor (1832-1905) Missionary to China

The church's AWANA display at Homecoming in Baltic, Ohio.

Brother Mike Ianniello shared the gospel at the Coshocton County Fair.

Teens and adults at Harvest Bonfire and Hayride.

A video was prepared for the 2011 Christmas Program.

Pastor Neal speaking at the Chili Church Daughter Banquet in 2011.

Daughter Banquet 2011 with 170 ladies in attendance.

The children are enjoying the sprinkler at the church's Community Cookout.

Presenting awards at the AWANA Closing Program in 2012.

The Chili Church teens and their leaders served for a day at the Haven of Rest Mission in Akron, Ohio.

Chili teens enjoying lunch at Haven of Rest Mission in Akron, Ohio.

Two of our teens cleaning chairs at Haven of Rest Mission in Akron, Ohio.

Scott Brillhart and Pastor Neal helping the teens at the Havem of Rest in Akron, Ohio.

Young people and their leaders standing in the snow outside the church bus on a cold winter day.

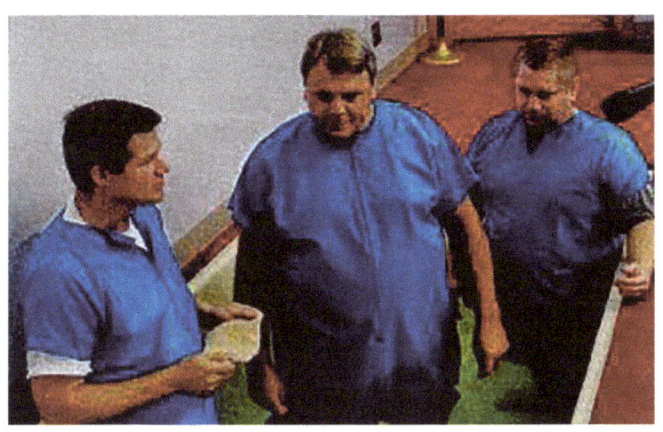

Pastor Neal prepares to baptize a new believer in the church's baptismal pool.

APPENDIX

The Original Charter Members of Chili Crossroads Bible Church (1953)

1. John Everhart
2. Mrs. John Everhart
3. Frank D. Fisher
4. Mrs. Ruth Fisher
5. Clarence H. Grogro
6. Helen Grogro
7. Mary Haines
8. Charles Hecker
9. Edwin Hothem
10. Esther Hothem
11. Clyde Huprich
12. Mary Huprich
13. Mrs. Mabel Huprich
14. Valentine Huprich
15. Harvey Kobel
16. Miriam Kobel
17. Rev. Owen Lower
18. Mrs. Thelma K. Lower
19. Cora McClure
20. Harry McClure
21. Theodore McQueen
22. Mrs. Theodore McQueen
23. Henry Mast
24. Mrs. Helen Mast
25. Mrs. Mellanie Mathias
26. Majorie A. Mathias
27. Lester R. Miller
28. Mrs. Lester R. Miller
29. Lucy C. Rice
30. Jim Edward Schlagenhauf
31. Amanda Stroup

EPILOGUE

Promoted To God's Heaven

JESUS said, "Today thou shall be with Me in Paradise." (Luke 23:43)

IN MEMORIAM

The Faithful Members and Friends of the Crossroads Bible Church, whose names are listed below, have been promoted — and are now with the **LORD** in **HIS** Heaven, where all born-again Christians will be with the **KING OF KINGS AND THE LORD OF LORDS** in the future:

- Duane L. Bacon (1934-2009)
- Marjorie Ann Snyder Bacon (1936-2012)
- Rev. James A. Boyd (1916-1987)
- ★ John W. Everhart (1911-1989)
- ★ Irene H. Everhart (1914-1997)
- ★ Clarence H. Grogro (1906-1994)
- ★ Mary Haines (1899-1967)
- Forest E. Harstine (1919-1995)
- ★ Charles Hecker (1877-1959)
- ★ Edwin Hothern (1899-1982)
- ★ Esther Hothern (1902-1995)
- ★ Clyde Huprich (1911-1984)
- ★ Mabel Huprich (1894-1992)
- ★ Mary Huprich (1915-2006)
- ★ Valentine Huprich (1876-1963)
- ★ Harvey Kobel (1908-1977)
- ★ Miriam Kobel (unavailable)
- Michael Lewis Ianniello (1953-2012)
- Elizabeth Levengood (1930-2011)
- ★ Rev. Owen E. Lower (1915-1999)
- ★ Thelma K. Lower (1909-2005)
- ★ Cora McClure (1895-1985)
- ★ Henry McClure (1888-1968)
- John E. McCrea (1930-2013)
- ★ Theodore J. McQueen (unavailable)
- ★ Mrs. Theodore J. McQueen (unavailable)
- Florence Magers (1918-1991)
- Glenn Parker Magers (1916-1981)
- ★ Henry A. Mast (1908-1979)
- ★ Helen E. Mast (1914-2008)
- ★ Mellanie I. Matthias (1909-1994)
- Rev. Daniel C. Meininger (1941-2007)
- ★ Helen E. Miller (1920-1997)
- ★ Lester R. Miller (1912-1974)
- Nellie Miller (not available)
- ★ Lucy R. Rice (1908-2003)
- Kenneth Eugene Schlarb (1927-2012)
- Marjorie A. Schlarb (1932-2013)
- Harold Schultz (not available)
- Amada Stroup (1881-not available)
- Alva Francis Tyson (1914-2010)
- Mary Tyson (1912-1997

(*Charter Members of Chili Crossroads Bible Church)

Well done, thou good and faithful servants, Enter thou into the Joy of thy Lord! Matthew 25:21

CONCLUSION

When the Revolutionary War in America ended in 1781, and its peace treaty, the Treaty of Paris of 1783, was signed, significant numbers of both Americans and Europeans settled in the Ohio Territory, which resulted in Ohio becoming the 17th State of the United States in 1803. Coshocton County was then organized in 1811 and Crawford Township was incorporated in 1828. A few years later, the Village of Chili within Crawford Township began in 1834. German settlers came to the Chili area, which led to the opening of three Protestant churches near Chili. Services in all three of these churches were conducted in the German Language. Chili reached its highest population in the early 1940's. But eventually the population of Chili decreased significantly, and all three of these churches permanently closed.

But in the wise Providence of God, one of these three churches, the St. John's German Evangelical Congregation Church of Chili, became the home of a new church organization, the Chili Crossroads Bible Church in 1952. Under the capable leadership of Rev. Owen E. Lower, the old church was reopened, a Sunday School was organized, a weekly Gospel radio broadcast began, and a Vacation Bible School for children was held each summer. Pastor and Mrs. Lower served both the Fresno Bible Church and Chili Crossroads Bible Church for nine years.

In 1961, Rev. James H. Boyd became the pastor of both the Fresno Bible Church and Chili Crossroads Bible Church, and along with his wife, he ministered to both congregations for thirteen years. Under his wise leadership these two churches became two separate independent churches in 1974. And then, Pastor and Mrs. Boyd devoted nine more years to the Chili church exclusively, concluding their fruitful ministry there in 1983.

From 1983 through 2004, the next five pastors of the Chili Crossroads Bible Church faithfully preached the Gospel, taught the Bible, ministered to the people, and promoted home and foreign missions, and in so doing, they built upon the solid foundation already laid by Pastor Lower and Pastor Boyd, and the church became a stronger vibrant Bible-believing church.

During the next five years (2004-2009), the Chili Crossroads Bible Church was greatly challenged by two significant needs: First, the church was not able to find a permanent full-time pastor, and secondly, its church building collapsed, and could not be rebuilt on the same site. But as the Chili Christians regularly and conscientiously met together and prayed for the needs of their church, the LORD met them at HIS Throne of Grace, and HE answered their prayers in His own unique and wonderful ways. The Congregation was able to purchase suitable land on which to build a new House of Worship, and a new church was built, fully paid for, and dedicated to the glory of God. And then the LORD provided Pastor Joseph and Barbara Essington from New Jersey to give the church pastoral leadership and encouragement, until the LORD sent Pastor and Mrs. Neal Dearyan from Illinois as a long-term and full-time pastoral couple to the church.

Pastor Neal and Julie Dearyan have been faithfully serving the LORD at Chili Crossroads Bible Church since September 2009. God is being glorified, people are being reached with the Gospel and coming to CHRIST in faith, while Christian believers are being baptized, edified, and encouraged. And the church is growing!

The LORD is abundantly blessing HIS Church at Chili. And although we do not know what the future may hold, we do know that. . .

JESUS <u>NEVER</u> FAILS!

BIBLIOGRAPHY

Boyd, Dorothea, A Brief History of the Chili Crossroads Bible Church, Chili, Ohio. The 100th Anniversary of the Building, 1870-1979, (6 pages, soft cover, 1979 (privately printed).

Crawford Township, Coshocton, Ohio. Cemeteries, History, Photos, Coshocton, Ohio, The Coshocton County Genealogical Society, 2001. (250 pages, soft cover).

Kirchenbuch (Church Book). The Evangelical Congregation of St. Johannes Church in Chili, Coshocton County, OH. Records from December 1st, 1879. As translated and copied by Maxine Renner Ebele, 1982. (28 pages, soft cover).

Kraybill, Donald B., Nolt, Steven M., Weaver-Zercher, David L., Amish Grace. How Forgiveness Transcended Tragedy San Francisco, CA: Jossey-Blasé, John Wiley & Sons, Inc. 2007. (237 pages, hard cover).

Nicholson, Roger S., TEMPORARY SHEPHERDS: A Congregational Handbook for Interim Ministry. An Alban Institute Publication, 1998. (205 pages, soft cover).

United States Atlas for Young Explorers, Third Edition. Washington, D.C.: National Geographic Society, 1985. (448 pages, hard cover).

Wright, Majorie A., VILLAGE OF CHILI, 2011. (140 pages, soft cover).

Pamphlets, Magazines, Newspapers:

Coshocton Tribune. Coshocton, OH (newspaper).

Valuable Internet Sources:

www.chilibiblechurch.org/
www.coshoctonlibrary.org.
www.familysearch.com.
www.qrbbc.org.
www.wikipedia.org.

ACKNOWLEDGMENTS

Written on the 61st Anniversary of the Chili Crossroads Bible Church (1953-2014) by Dr. A. Joseph Essington

THANK YOU TO ALL THOSE WHO CONTRIBUTED PICTURES, NAMES, AND OTHER INFORMATION, AND ESPECIALLY TO MRS. BARBARA McMASTERS, WHO GENEROUSLY SHARED HER PHOTOGRAPHIC COLLECTION WITH THE AUTHOR.

The author also wishes to express his heartfelt gratitude to Angie Brillhart, Julie Dearyan, Ruth Hall, and Parker C. Thompson, for proofreading and making valuable suggestions.

And to Denis P. Humphreys and Camille Walker, for their technical assistance, and a special word of thanks to Kari Kumura, for her work in designing the book's cover.

INDEX

A

Alexander, John, 6
American Indians, 4, 5
Arizona College of the Bible, 24
Awana, 44, 45, 48

B

Baltic, 7, 34, 45
Baptism, 10, 41
Bauer, Rev. David J., 33
Bavaria, 7
Benchmark, 8
Bible Christian Union, 14, 16
Bible Hour, 15
Bible Related Ministries, Inc., 33
Blue Jacket, 5
Bob Jones University, 21
Boyd, Dorthea, 19
Boyd, John, 20
Boyd, Rev. James H., 17, 19, 20, 52
Boyd, Tim, 20
Buckongahelas, 5

C

Charter Members, 16, 50, 51
Chili Crossroads Bible Church Cemetery, 12
Chili Methodist Episcopal Church, 7
Chili Schoolhouse, 9
Chili Village, 7
Chili, Coshocton County, Ohio, 9
Christmas Party, 46
Coates, Dale Family, 34
Communism, 10
Community Cookout, 47
Coshocton County, 1, 5, 7, 8, 52, 54
Coshocton County Bookmobile, 35
Coshocton County Fair, 45
Crawford Township, 1, 2, 5, 6, 15, 52, 54
Cutshall, Rev. Chris, 24

D

Daughter Banquet, 46
Dearyan, Julie, 2, 37, 38, 41, 42, 43, 44, 53, 55
Dearyan, Neal, 42, 43, 44, 52, 53
Deceased Members and Friends, 51

E

Essington, Barbara, 34, 36, 52
Essington, Rev. A. Joseph, 2, 33, 35, 36, 40, 55
Evangelical Alliance Mission, 23

F

Fairfield Cemetery, 10, 16
Faith Baptist Church, 22
Fallen Timbers, Battle of, 5
Fensler, John, 6
Fensler, Magdalene, 6
Fensler, Philip, 6
Fensler, Samuel, 6
Fiat, 7
Fresno Bible Church, 14, 15, 16, 17, 18, 24, 52
Fresno Farmers Market, 36
Fresno Public School, 26

G

German Language, 7, 9, 52
German Reformed Church, 9
Germany, 7, 10
Goodrich, Dorthea, 17
Grace Bible College, 23
Grace Theological Seminary, 33
Grand Rapids School of the Bible and Music, 23
Great Depression, 10

H

Haefelle, Rev. F. M., 9
Harvest Bonfire and Hayride, 45
Haven of Rest Mission, 43, 49
Horsfall, Rev. Ned, 22, 24

I

I.G.A. Store, 6, 7
Ianniello, Michael Lewis, 51
Ignite Summer Youth Group, 44
Illinois, State of, 4, 17, 23, 33, 37, 38, 41, 52
In Memoriam, 51

J

Jesus Never Fails, 35, 43, 53

K

Kaiser, Rev. Daniel M., 22, 23, 24
Kandel, Pastor John D., 25, 29
Kent State University, 22
Kirchenbuch, 9, 10, 54
Klassett, Thelma L., 14

L

Land Ordinance of 1785, 4
Leindecker, Myron and Cora, 15
Lorenz, John and Margaret, 9
Lower, Rev. Owen E., 14, 16, 21, 43, 50, 51, 52

M

Macy, Rev. David C., 24, 25
Maumee River, 5
McAuley Water Street Mission, 33
McMasters, Barbara, 55
Meininger, Carolyn, 22, 23
Meininger, Rev. Daniel C., 22, 25, 51
Michigan, State of, 4, 22, 23
Miller, Mike, 30
MMS Aviation, 34
Moody Bible Institute, 17, 25

Mount Zion Lutheran Church, 6, 7
Mullins, Rev. Randy, 21, 24

N

Nazi Germany, 10
New Bedford, 5
New Jersey, State of, 2, 23, 33, 34, 38, 41, 52
Newcomerstown, 16
Northwest Ordinance, 4
Northwest Territory, 4

O

Ohio Dutch Construction Company, 28
Ohio River, 1, 4, 5
Ohio Territory, 1, 52
Ohio, State of, 1, 2, 3, 4, 5, 7, 18

P

Palmer, Rev. George A., 35
Pennsylvania Germans, 5
Pete's Inn and Gas Station, 6
Philadelphia College of Bible, 24
Priest, Jim, 30

Q

Quentin Road Bible Baptist Church, 37, 38, 39, 41, 42

R

Radio Station WTNS, 15, 33, 34
Ragersville, 7
Ravenscraft, James, 6
Revolutionary War (1775-1783), 1, 3, 4, 52
Rhode Island, State of, 4
Roberts, Charles Carl, IV, 27
Rockenhausen, 7

S

Salem County Correctional Facility, 33
Scudder, Dr. James A., 38

Shanesville, 7
Shelton College, 33
St. John's German Evangelical Church Congregation of Chili, Coshocton County, Ohio, 15
Sunday School, 9, 15, 23, 36, 37, 52

T

Talbot Theological Seminary, 24
TalkTime, 44
Tennessee Temple University, 22
Treaty of Fort Stanwix, 5
Treaty of Greenville, 5
Treaty of Paris (1783), 1, 3, 4, 5, 52
Trieste, Italy, 23
Troyer, Anna Mae, 26
Troyer, Henry M., 27
Troyer, Robert M., 26, 27

U

United States Geological Society, 8

W

Waldgrehweiler, 7
Washington, President George, 4
Wayne, General "Mad" Anthony, 4
West Lafayette, 16, 24
West Nickel Mines School, 27
Western Frontier, 4
Wheaton College, 14, 17
White Eyes Township, 6
Wisconsin, State of, 4
Wright, Marjorie A., 10

Y

Yorktown, VA, 3

www.ingramcontent.com/pod-product-compliance
Lightning Source LLC
LaVergne TN
LVHW070534070526
838199LV00075B/6776